I0622897

A Pandemic
Gardening Journal

Conover Lane LLC.
Pennsylvania, USA
For more information, check out conoverln.com

A Pandemic Gardening Journal

Matt Puchalski

Thank you Mary K. Donnelly for your editing and support.

TABLE OF CONTENTS

TOP-DOWN VIEW OF THE HOUSE

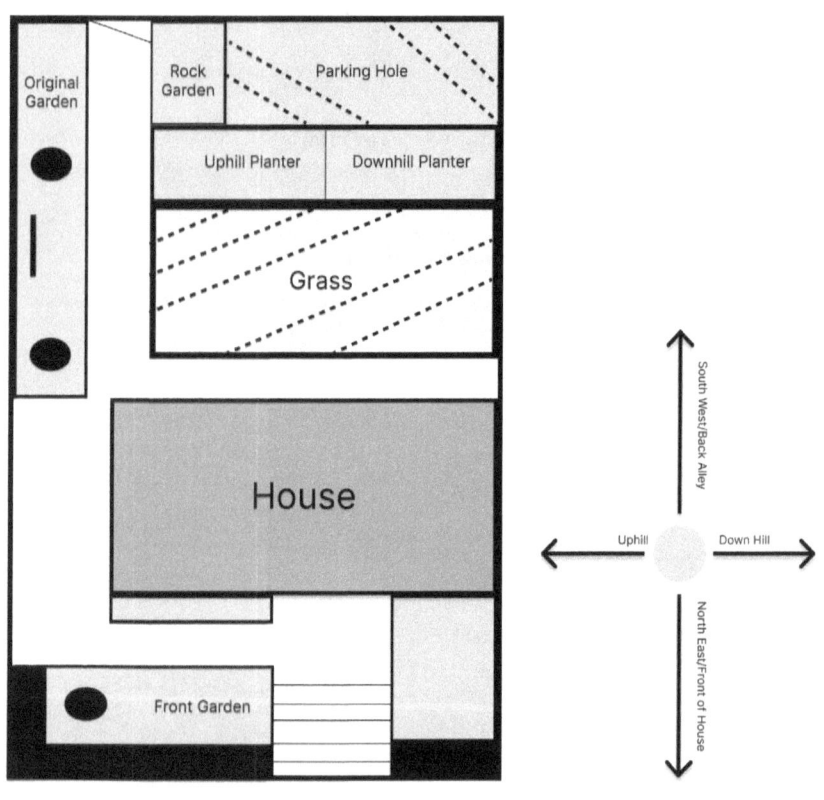

PROLOGUE

February 2023, and I'm in New York City avoiding a rainstorm. It's getting late and when there's a break in the clouds, I decide to move a few blocks from the Starbucks I'm working from to find a new coffee shop. A few months earlier had seen the company I was working for collapse, and I was lucky enough to start working right away on a new project. With this change, most of my days were spent on Zoom or drafting new documents, both of which can be done remotely; I packed up and headed to New Jersey to spend some time with family before the physical work kicked in and I needed to be on-site.

When I stepped into the new coffee shop I discovered the Espresso Book Machine at Shakespeare & Co on Lexington Avenue in Manhattan. The machine sits in the middle of this college bookstore/cafe and looks like a large ink-jet printer. Intrigued by the idea of being able to print a book on demand, I took a flyer from the desk it sat on and moved on down the road to meet my brother for an early dinner at an Irish pub near where he works. It was sitting at this bar on this wet wintry day I had the idea to write about my time gardening. A few weeks later, and I had my first draft completed.

PART I :
A BACKGROUND

1. MY GARDENING BACKGROUND

Growing up in New Jersey, gardening was a as thrilling as a trip to the dentist, or being dragged along to my sister's dance classes. Actually, both of those activities were more thrilling to me because at least you could read while you wait. Because New Jersey is the "Garden State," I connected the word gardening to what was around me: large fields of grass for horse farms broken up by occasional forests, orchards, or corn fields that then abutted abruptly into cookie cutter housing developments and their smaller dollops of grass. That we lived in the smack middle of the state only solidified the association

garden = grass

My memories of working in parents' quarter-acre yard revolve heavily around the maintenance and upkeep of the lawn. This was a matter of practicality as my siblings and I used every inch of the front and back yard as play areas. Alongside the rest of the neighborhood children, we'd take turns churning up a new lawn a day depending on the mood, weather, and everyone's availability to play. To us, going out into your parents' yard and picking up sticks after a storm wasn't a chore to be checked off a list, it was a near patriotic duty to your fellow children because you knew they were doing the same thing. Rakes, shovels, and shears were our instruments, and we all had a particular favorite for its own reasons. My brother loved the lightweight spade shovel while I could use a transfer shovel for days without stopping. The faster you got your yard taken care of, the faster you could dash down the street, lend a hand and a rake, and complete the ritual at the neighbor's house.

This was to us as "gardening" and something I didn't fully grasp until I got older, when the tools of the trade upgraded from rakes and tarps to heavy equipment.

When I was 10, I received my first pair of steel-toed boots. The same year, we upgraded the lawn mower from an ancient machine to a new-to-us John Deere riding mower. My father scoured eBay for months looking for the exact right deal, and we found it in the two-year old tractor a family a few towns over had purchased before realizing that one of the natural predators of a riding lawnmower is a turf on a mild incline.

The steel-toed boots were a ritual; if I was outside and there was work to be done, the boots were on. This association of yard work and safety equipment pleased my parents, and definitely prevented a few missing toes as I grew beyond the riding mower and on to the weed whacker, edger, and snow plow, but is an association I keep to this day. I've had a pair of work boots in my parents' garage — just in case — since I first moved out for college.

My association of work boots and outdoor work also extended to the inner perimeter of the yard: the flowers that immediately surrounded the house, and the folding-table sized plot immediately outside of the kitchen dedicated to herbs and tomatoes. I'd wear my boots to weed some corner of the flowers, never fully understanding what was a weed and what wasn't. Once when I was 17 I was put in charge of the yearly tomato seedling order from the local garden supply store. I was instructed to, "buy three and make sure they look healthy." Being a unit-less order of, "three," I bought three flats of the best looking seedlings they had and brought them home, covering every inch of the family minivan in potting soil in the process. You can imagine the look on everyone's face at the **fifty-four** tomato seedlings I acquired. I went door to door in the neighborhood giving out the extra seedlings and our aunts and uncles took a few, but not a single family gathering goes by without someone inevitably deriding me for my lack of gardening awareness.

2. HOUSE AND HOME

A fter 18 months in Pittsburgh, I was committed to my new home. Work was exciting, I no longer navigated the city entirely based on Google Maps, and I was tired of my apartment. My apartment was the first place I had lived alone. Located in Pittsburgh's trendy Lawrenceville neighborhood, it was on the third floor of an old Boys & Girls Club that was converted to a mixed apartment/retail space. I signed the apartment lease sight unseen, but I was moving in the middle of winter and was aware of Pittsburgh's reputation for hills and that gave me an icy anxiety. A bad apartment I could deal with, but a bad apartment at the top of a hill I imagined my old car wouldn't be able to get up or down safely? Unacceptable.

Since the new company was based in the adjoining neighborhood of the Strip District, I knew I'd be able to walk to and from work on snowy days. As luck would have it, I was the first person to rent in this "new" building and as such, locked in a terrific deal on the rent.

I fell in love with my new slice of the world. Located in Western Pennsylvania, Pittsburgh is an old city with industrial beginnings. Geographically, Pittsburgh is set in the confluence of three rivers: the Allegheny, the Ohio, and the Monongahela. These rivers and their ancient progenitors carved the region into hills and valleys that gives the area a timeless quality. Seen from above via airplane or intimately close while hiking, one can lose a sense of whether they're still in the US or if they've stepped into France's Alsace or an Irish shire.

Anthropologically, Pittsburgh is a richly diverse city with 90 neighborhoods. These districts each have their own cultural roots and historical reasons for being, and often follow the geography of the city. The neighborhood of Polish Hill is, as one could expect, a residential community settled by Polish immigrants and occupies a large hill in the center of the city.

Located on the south bank of the Allegheny River, my neighborhood of Lawrenceville is bounded to the east by the cemetery and rises gently (for Pittsburgh) from the river to crest at the Children's Hospital. The main artery of the neighborhood, Butler Street, follows the ambles of the Allegheny at a set-back deep enough that local business has thrived in recent years. Butler street is the point the hill truly begins, and that's where most of the residents of the neighborhood reside. It was this hill that I focused my home search to: an area that roughly encompasses one half of one square mile.

Most of Lawrenceville's homes were constructed between 1870 and 1940. During this seventy-year period, Lawrenceville boomed with the rest of Pittsburgh as the steel and oil industries created immense wealth and brought millions of people to the area. Because of this industrialization, Lawrenceville transitioned from a collection of small farms to a district for the working class. Single-family homes went up block by block. This period was also one of incredible modernization and standardization. Houses built before the discovery of electricity sit next to those that not only were built after electrification, but who still hold their original General Electric appliances purchased by the first homeowner and still in active operation.

It's this industrialist charm that so deeply appealed to me. Lawrenceville is a neighborhood of long timers, and there's been an influx of new people moving to the neighborhood alongside me. While there's an allure in the convenience of the modern, the charm of history drew me to finding a house with good bones that I could add to its character instead of encouraging the convergence to conformity.

After several months of house hunting, I found my home in a brick house built in 1920. The sellers had been in the house for roughly five years, and in that time had upgraded the electrical and replaced the air conditioning in addition to some interior painting, but that was essentially all they did. They had purchased the house from an old woman who had spent her entire life in the place. Her parents purchased the home from the builder and according to legend were given the choice of either this house or its mirror a few doors up the hill. Since it was uncouth at the time to be known as living on the top of the hill, they chose to be as close to the river as possible. Depending on how you count it, I'm either the third or fourth owner of an over 100 year-old property, and a poll of my neighbors shows that is roughly the standard.

I signed the paperwork to the house on May 31, and turned 25 on my first full day of homeownership.

3. THE FIRST FEW MONTHS

The move into my new home went by in a blur. Because my apartment was down the hill I moved in dribs and drabs, assessing this purchase of mine and transitioning everything to my new permanent residence. It was the middle of summer and everything came to the house one Mercury Milan trunkload at a time. Keeping with the house's theme of, "old," I U-Haul trucked my grandmother's dining room set to my new home. It was incredible to have my brother and his college friends onsite to do the heavy lifting for the low price of

pizza and beer. To me it was the peace of mind to not have to worry about hauling a couch up two flights of stairs; to them it was a cheap meal and I sent them home with the leftovers.

I set to work making mistakes and surveying every inch of the home. The dining room's accent wall was a shade of orange that made everyone who walked through the room take on a Velma-esque glow. Tackling this wall was my first foray into an element of homeownership that is not my strong suit: interior painting, but in replacing the wall I now have a dining room I enjoy sitting in, so a win is a win.

The front of the house is approximately fifteen feet higher than street level. This rise is split between a few outdoor steps that then split off to a concrete walkway that wraps around to the back of the house. Climbing further to the front door takes you to the front porch, a spacious place to take in the view of every other neighbor's front porch. Because of the front walkway, the front of the house is broken into three small gardening beds.

The front garden's most striking feature is the hedge row that rings the large bed. These hedges are original to the construction of the house and its neighbors also featured hedges at construction, but over time my house is the only one that kept this original feature. From the street, the hedges give a sense of privacy, but it's what the hedges block in that is their strongest appeal to me. Looking down from the front porch onto the hedges takes the eye to an unassuming patch of earth, and a small and rather dirty looking tree. The tree became a, "future me" problem, and I decided to place some seemingly innocuous bulbs into this plot. In the coming years, that first planting of daylillies and daffodils would be a near infinite source of joy while sitting on the front porch, and that dirty tree would yield wonders.

The rear features a small porch that squares off the house at the kitchen, a patch of grass roughly thirty five feet long by thirty feet across, and street level parking. To achieve this, the yard drops off a rather dramatic 10 feet to meet the alley below, and a shotgun of steps takes you from the street to the grass. Originally the on street parking was a covered garage, but nearly 20 years ago the roof of the garage collapsed and instead of a replacement, the rubble was scattered about the yard or smuggled out into the weekly garbage collection and forgotten. In the most grand fashion I could muster, I began calling the place I'd overnight my car the "parking hole," since it couldn't reasonably be called a garage and the street level to backyard level difference is roughly 12 feet.

On my first rainy day of homeownership, I slipped in the mud while bringing in groceries up through the alley. The next morning I tripped at the exact same spot while attempting to leave for work. Stopping to inspect the site, I realized there was a brick sticking out of the earth and that was what I'd tripped over. As my eyes followed the flow the mud took on its way to the alley, I discovered a brick walkway covered by an inch of topsoil. I took this as an opportunity to visit the neighborhood hardware store, the Busy Beaver, and excitedly purchased a hand trowel and hand rake.

The next sunny evening I took hand tools to the earth and started probing. Laying on my stomach, prodding the earth like a mine sweeper one hand trowel poke at a time, I edged out the shape of the pathway. Prizing the earth up from this edging, I was able to roll up a carpet of earth with a fully intact, period walkway there to greet me. Completing this well after sundown, I pushed my sod into a corner of the yard and triumphed in my brick-based discovery. Looking back, I rolled up nearly 45 square feet of beautiful compost that could have accelerated any number of new plant-based projects, but I wouldn't cross over to a true obsessive for a little while longer.

My fear of what the loose brick in the soil meant was based in pragmatism. Pittsburgh had been through some hard times through the life of the house, and long-time residents have many stories about the period of long time decay that was most aggressive from the 1960s through the early 2000s. When speaking to coworkers about the property, I was instructed to ask if the house had ever had a septic system. Being in the middle of the city I thought that was absurd, but because of how quickly Pittsburgh expanded then shrunk septic was a common practice at the time the house was built because the city could not guarantee access to public utilities in time for people to move in. Houses would eventually be converted over to public sewers, at which point the septic tanks would sit in peoples yards untouched. Companies have popped up offering to dig out tanks in the hopes of speculating on their contents — for as long as there have been people, there have been people losing things down the drain. While there was no septic on the property or on the street, I did notice more and more bits of concrete around the yard.

As it turns out, the remnants of the garage were still onsite. Within the first two weeks of ownership, I tackled a huge clump of weedy, tall grass in the very back corner of the yard. In Link-like fashion the hack and slash revealed a secret; though neither rupees or treasure chests met me after my labors, I did find a few hundred pounds of concrete sitting on the dirt. At my present rate of one Target trip per day, I would have preferred a treasure chest.

When I asked the neighbor across the street why no one had dealt with the weeds before, he said that everyone thought they looked better than a big pile of concrete and moved on with life. Pittsburgh.

When I asked the neighbor across the street why no one had dealt with the weeds before, he said that everyone thought they looked better than a big pile of concrete and moved on with life. Pittsburgh.

I was now fully moved into the house, and was comfortable with my surroundings. Fall was rapidly approaching, and with that a rapid blast into Pittsburgh winter. I acquired an electric lawnmower and weed whacker set, selecting these particular models because they were the same brand of battery charger as my power drill. Now a pro at navigating the Busy Beaver, I upsized the hand trowel to purchase myself a spade and flathead shovel, a hedge trimmer, and a pair of cattleman gloves.

Every weekend I'd do a quick lap with the lawnmower. Occasionally I'd notice a flake of concrete peak through the grass, but I would write it off as a rock of some kind. After the lawnmower, I'd move to trim the front hedges by hand in an insane act of "yard maintenance." This act of kaiju-sized bonsai left me exhausted to attempt any more complex yard acts, but it did give me time to ponder the control a hand tool can provide. I've been shaving my head daily for the last five years so I barely remember a barbershop experience, but it's the closest I've come to understanding the difference between when to use scissors vs. a buzzer.

"I'll figure it out during winter" I'd tell myself. I focused on setting up the inside of the house, painting and purchasing furniture and cleaning and unboxing. What I could not account for what that winter would bring a new need to pay attention to my backyard. As the calendar turned to 2020 I, like the rest of the world, suddenly spent a large amount of time staring out the window and thinking about our place in the world.

PART II :
THE FIRST YEAR

4. WINTER

W ith the global pandemic of March 2020 came a focus on the personal. Work moved to fully remote so my commute, like billions around the world, shifted one fully confined to home. I became acutely aware of how lucky I was to have the luxury of space in the form my my back yard. At a time when people were disinfecting groceries for fear of the unknown, I'd sit and ponder how I could improve my workspace and back yard.

The basement was a part of the house I'd made great improvements to, and was my primary base of operations for all of my engineering works. Even though the house had a 200A electrical panel, the basement was lit by one lightbulb on either end of the space, and had exactly two outlets. With my dad, we improved the space dramatically by installing outlets at even intervals on all of the walls and replacing the morose lighting for a smattering of LED shop lights.

One of my proudest moments of basement design came when I purchased my washer and dryer. For the first 80 years of the home, all laundry was done using a hand-powered wash tub with clothing hung on a clothesline in the backyard to dry. Jumping to the 21st century, an electric single unit washer/dryer combo unit was installed in the basement, but this left with the previous sellers. Conveniently, the house has a laundry shoot from the second floor straight to the basement. Its dark wood and brass latch give a quaint pop of the antique to my living space, but the business end in the basement served as my ideal resting place for a clothes washer. The weird peace of mind I receive every time I hurl clothes straight from the hallway outside my bedroom straight into the washing machine is indescribable.

Opposite the washer/dryer was a bare wall, and being in need of a project, I stared at that bare wall until an idea hit me. On a laundry day, I noticed my gardening supplies had shifted and were strewn about. Up to this point my yard tools were overwintering in a corner of the basement, and it appeared they fell apart some time in the preceding week. While tidying everything back into its corner, bending over to grab at the tools, I misstepped and Sideshow Bob-ed myself with my spade shovel, popping myself in the nose with the shovel handle. While embarrassing, this was the inspiration for a project I required.

With two pieces of spare wood, some concrete screws, and a peg board, I found a new home for my outdoor tools, and a project that occupied an afternoon.

Gaining some confidence in my organizational abilities, my gaze again turned to the back yard. Although it was a mild winter, it was winter nonetheless, and I didn't know if I could really do anything botanical, so I settled on cleaning up the concrete.

After picking through the mess, it was largely a collection of whole and partial cinderblocks, some concrete hunks, and bits of bricks, alongside some classic broken glass and detritus. I dubbed this part of the yard the, "rock garden," and began toying with the idea I'd make some kind of sculpture out of my pile of junk.

I, like much of the world, drifted through a baking phase at this time and was producing a loaf of some kind of bread every day or so. The "best" result I had, an soda bread using a recipe passed down to me from an Irish nun who taught me in grade school, wasn't close to what it tasted like in memories. The story gives the bread its flavor and not the baker so I looked for ways to give my baking its own identity. Driven by desires for new spice, I scrapped the idea for a sculpture and decided to reclaim the rock garden as the site of a container garden.

With the idea of a container garden rumbling around, I next needed to figure out what to do with my bits of construction debris. I could attempt to Great Escape the rubble out bit by bit in the trash, but that would take who knows how long, and I still wanted to put it to some sort of use. In an attempted homage to Pittsburgh's industrial roots, I decided I had enough material in the rock garden to edge a brand new planter. My plot of grass is already closer to a postage stamp than anything I would have called a yard as a child, so scraping away some more of the grass wouldn't bruise any pretense of a suburban ego.

Starting with the most "complete" cinder block and brick, I traced out a planter following the edge of the parking hole. When I had barely made a dent in the prettiest pieces of rubble, one planter became two; I would go on to re-edge the walkway from the alley to the yard, complete those two planters, and have enough bits of concrete left to stack into a pile I have lied to myself to the point of calling it, "art."

With a re-edged back walkway and a rock garden sans rubble, I had a foundation for my container garden. After some meticulous internet-searching, I discovered there is a big difference in cost and quality in pots that are indoor only or indoor/outdoor. The reason being indoor/outdoor needing to go through much more aggressive temperature swings than the containers of the domestic variety. Another fun internet tip is that it's always worth the extra few pennies to get a container with existing drain holes. Searching high and low, I found unreasonably good deals on containers at my local Home Goods store. Apparently, the best time of year to buy outdoor features is in the winter when no one else is buying.

While turning over the earth for the planters, I made an unpleasant but not surprising discovery: the entire yard is sprinkled with rubble. This started as novelty, then became good exercise, but now it's a reminder of the past. Every winter brings a freeze and thaw cycle, and that cycle brings fresh concrete closer to the surface. My avant garde planters complete, they now yearned to be occupied.

5. SPRING

Infinite possibilities stared at me as I began dreaming about April showers and May flowers. My private oasis in the front of the house would be untouched this first growing season. I told myself I was attempting to keep up with my forebears. "Everyone who's been there has kept the front up," I'd hear, usually followed by, "though of course there was a long stretch when things were left on their own." Leaving things on their own for one more season wouldn't hurt anything, and I wanted to see what came up.

At the rear of the house, I also had a few elements of the yard I knew I wouldn't be touching any time soon. The rose and sage bushes were to remain, as was the brain-looking clump next to the sage. These brains growing out of the ground were the beginnings of rhubarb! Seriously, rhubarb is such an incredibly funky plant and something I would have never thought to plant if it wasn't already there. Prolific and fascinating, this sweet perennial has basically zero pests and expands slowly and via rhizome — like grasses or strawberries, rhubarb's grows year after year underground, out and then up.

After its brain phase, rhubarb dramatically folds out into celery like stalks with palm tree-like leaves and then goes into overdrive producing sugar. When it turns a deep pink/red, the rhubarb is ready for harvesting. A mild winter coupled with a personal lack of understanding on how broad a growing season can be meant that I was incredibly surprised when my rhubarb hit its prime the first week of April.

With a clean pair of scissors I harvested the rhubarb starting a few centimeters off the ground. I knew I should put it to good use, and I figured no one would complain if I messed anything up, so I hopped on the internet and started reading about what I could bumble myself through, so rhubarb pie was immediately out. What *was* within my self-perceived capabilities was an infused simple syrup. Sugar, water, mason jars, and the rhubarb itself was all it took, and the recipe I followed can be found at the end of this book. The mason jars were a bit tough to acquire, but I found a flat of 4 oz. jelly jars at the hardware store that worked perfectly.

WOW! That syrup was incredible. Rhubarb syrup-drizzled oatmeal for breakfast, infused lemonade for lunch, and tart pink Manhattans became my staples. Refrigerated 4 ounces at a time, I had more syrup than I knew what to do with, so I packed up a few kits and distributed them to my next door neighbors. The uphill four-year-old and my ninety-year-old downhill neighbor agreed: I had hit upon a universally agreed upon pick-me-up.

Roses are red,

Sage grows in a bush,

Rhubarb is tart,

A unique, tangy rush.

Spring in Pittsburgh is really a continuation of winter with a quick smack in the face to summer, so I was spending virtually every moment indoors with a quick dash to the mailbox each evening. On one such jaunt, I discovered a collection of mason jars with a note from my neighbor, thanking me for the rhubarb syrup and encouraging me to make use of what she thought of as clutter from her basement. While haunting the halls of my house looking for a place to store these glassy treasures, I realized there was an extraordinary amount of well-lit interior space I could utilize. The sun reflecting off the metallic tops of the jars and into the antique crystalline structure was a welcome distraction, a DIY kaleidoscope distracting me from how little we knew about COVID-19 and my dread of whether or not I should bleach this neighborly gift. As quickly as the light caught my eye I was enraptured by how the late-afternoon sun felt falling through my kitchen window. The combination of the warmth and the light gave me an idea, and I squirreled the Mason jars in a hallway corner and followed the sun. From the hallway to the kitchen, up the stairs and into my southern-facing spare bedroom. The light faded and night came, but I was inspired.

With my interior space and the surplus of natural light on my mind, I decided to take on some roommates. I started spending more and more time in my guest bedroom. Its warmth and light made it the perfect reading paradise, and for the next few days I became a house cat. I'd position myself in a corner of the room and read until the light shifted, then I'd walk two steps, lay in the sun on the bed and nap in the sun until the light shifted again. Repeat until sundown. This time made me familiar with the room and helped me understand the roommates I had on the way who were to occupy this room.

Seeds make great roommates during a global pandemic. They stick to their room, never use all the hot water, and if you maintain your relationship with them, make excellent company in the kitchen. Their biggest drawback is how needy they are when they first move in — that and they are not great conversationalists.

Watching a few hours of YouTube videos and navigating as much of the gardening Reddit page I could, I started learning the vocabulary and "required" tools to take seeds from tiny bits of seeming dross to the beautiful backyard companions I yearned for. My first critical vocabulary word was

Growing Zone: the standard by which gardeners and growers can determine which plants are most likely to thrive at a location. Zones are displayed on a map and are based on the average annual minimum winter temperature, divided into 10-degree F zones.

Pittsburgh is located in growing zone *6b*. The scale runs from a frigid *1a* with its winter temperature range of *-60 to -55 °F (I cannot fathom a cold this consistent)* to the insane hot of zone *13b* and its winter minimum of *65 to 70 °F (the key word here being **minimum.**)* The city itself changes my growing zone from that of my suburban colleagues. It's not the largest metropolis but Pittsburgh is a big enough urban heat island that I'm measurably warmer than friends six miles away — just another example of how we shape our environment.

Temperature is a huge factor in determining if a plant has any chance at all of growing in a given area — this is why you see things like greenhouses, hothouses, and orangeries seen more often in colder climates — and because humans are obsessed with measuring temperature, it's a great first thing to check when deciding if a plant can grow where you are without some meddling.

Another important environmental component of plant selection comes in understanding the orientation of your yard, and what features naturally occur around the home. The front of my house faces north-east, and is packed in relatively closely to the neighboring houses. Because of shadows from my neighbors, my front "yard" gets small amounts of direct sunlight in the brightest of summer months. This is great when I'm sitting on the front porch attempting to cool off after a morning spent working in the yard, but it means that really sun-loving plants are off the table for these parts, and I can have a difficult time draining the yard after a heavy rainstorm.

With the back yard, the challenge comes in selecting plants that won't fry in the sun. Though the back yard faces an alley, my immediate neighbors on either side have flat yards similar to mine, meaning I have huge amounts of direct sunlight. Being in the middle of a hill and the south-west orientation of the yard, I lose out on the first few minutes of sun every morning as the light crests over the hill, and I lose light a few minutes earlier than I would in a flat city as the light passes behind my neighbors' houses. There are lots of plants that love the "give me all the light" I can naturally provide, but there are others where this can pose a problem. Through trial and error and learning some tricks I've been able to grow some plants that I'd otherwise avoid at first glance.

Ambient temperature and sunlight, those are the only elements that big ball of gas in the sky can influence in plant selection, right? Nope!

Soil temperature is a critical component of successful growing, but is far from a dealbreaker. I spent most of my life knowing very little of Pittsburgh, but the one thing I knew about the city was that it's cold. Pittsburgh is located south of Lake Erie, one of North America's Great Lakes. This proximity to the massive body of fresh water, coupled with the city's northern latitude means that every year our soil freezes during the coldest winter months. This freeze is actually a natural feature that some plants rely on to trigger dormancy period, that's followed by a growth period when things thaw. Plants that grow from bulbs — like my front yard's daylillies and daffodils — are the examples of plants that need cold ground temperatures to stay perennial, and their reliance on the thaw also makes them excellent symbols for springtime.

Spring doesn't just bring perennial flowers, it brought my first window to grow outdoor plants in the new year. As some plants need a freeze to trigger the start of their sprouting cycle, lots of plants have an internal switch to take them from, "keep making green bits," to, "it's getting hot in here, better start making some seeds." In broad strokes, plants sense this as a function of ground temperature, and when it happens "on schedule" you're a brilliant urban farmer who picked the right time to plant an early crop and harvested in time, and when you waited too long to plant or it's a warm spring and you don't get what you want out of the plant and it "goes to bolt," it's not a great feeling. I've experienced both sides of this, as have untold millions of people since the birth of farming, and I hope that you give it a go, too.

As an urban gardener, this temperature/seed relationship is something that I really love. I began to convert my guest bedroom into the world's worst greenhouse. This was at a time people were still figuring out how many masks on at the same time was the right amount of masks, so I didn't expect much in the way of company.

Planting a garden from seed, in spring, in Pittsburgh, means you have two choices in your selection: indirect and direct sowing. Indirect sowing is a process where you buy seeds, pop them in dirt or some other medium, then at a later date you transfer the resulting small plant or seedling to its final resting place. Direct sowing is exactly what it sounds like: when you think the time is right, and following the instructions on the back of the seed pack, you plop your seeds into your garden, cover them and wait for the magic to happen. Given a whole bedroom to play with, and my barren planters the bedroom looked down upon, I decided I'd attempt both indirect and direct sow plants this first spring.

Not all seeds are the same, and this is especially true when factoring in how long it takes for a plant to reach its maturity. This can be thought of as the average amount of time it takes a plant to go from "seed in the ground" to "plant ready for prime time." For things like vegetables, this means you're ready to eat, and for flowers it's an estimate of when the plant has reached it's peak "wow" time. When you do a poor job keeping track of where things are planted and what their maturity times are, it can lead to a bit of a nightmare as you plant things on top of each other, never quite sure what's a weed and what's intentionally there. When performed properly, it's an amazing feeling to harvest something then immediately know there's a plant that you've chosen waiting to fill that freshly opened soil.

This takes us to the critical element of seed selection: picking plants that you think are fun! You're purposely bringing life into the world. You've chosen to change your surroundings, and starting a garden from seed is a heavier mental commitment than letting your space go free or by starting a garden from starter plants. Because you're starting from seed, there's a much broader array of opportunities available to you and your garden than there would be if you let nature run its course or if you limited yourself to only gardening from full plants.

So, with all of these factors in mind, I selected my first plants to grow. Hopping onto Google, I searched, "best plant seeds online" and found a company I'd heard of before - Burpee. Founded in 1876 as a mail-order chicken business in Philadelphia, I thought the longevity of the brand meant they'd shipped through worse global situations, and their Philadelphia roots convinced me they'd probably have one or two plants I'd be able to grow in Pittsburgh. Not knowing how much anything would cost, I set a budget for myself that I wouldn't spend more than $75 in seeds and supplies this first order. Where that number came from, I couldn't tell you, but I can tell you I dramatically overestimated the cost of seeds.

Knowing I wanted some plants I could start indoors as well as straight in the ground, I gravitated mostly towards seeds with short growing cycles, and some really long term options just to see if I could handle it. Trawling the Burpee website, I ran through my list of factors to consider, and if I found a plant that made it all the way to the "fun" stage, I added a link to a running spreadsheet and moved on to the next plant on the site. In subsequent years, I'd learn a physical catalog is a much better medium than a few hundred tabs. Technology does not always equal progress. So with spreadsheet on screen, I Marie Kondo'd my way through each line asking if what I could grow would inspire joy. For those that survived the cut, I was back on Burpee's website to crowdsource what was the my best option in each category, looking for seed packets with over 50 reviews that were rated 4.5 stars or above.

With what seemed like limiting myself, I purchased one seed packet of the following:

Cucumbers
Sweet Peppers
Pole Beans
Pumpkins
French Breakfast Radishes
Daikon Radishes

Sunflowers

Tomatoes

Viewing my cart total, this barely cost $36, not even half of my $75 initial budget. There are much better deals to be found elsewhere, but this was a safe introduction to the hobby. With the funds I'd already mentally written off, I snagged two seed starting kits. If you've ever purchased a packet of six tomato seedlings at a big box store, this is basically what I'm talking about sans tomato seedling. As the name implies, a seed starting kit gives you everything you need to have an easy time in the early days of seed growing. There are tons of DIY options and these are as reusable as you make them, but the kit I went with had a base layer for watering, cell dividers to keep your plants separate, some "growth pellets," and a clear lid so you've basically got a greenhouse the size of a pizza box. I hit complete on my order and a few days later I had a manila envelope of seed packets and a box-of-boxes waiting on my front porch.

Headed to the basement, I began my seed starter kit journey. With something like 150 cells at my disposal, I thought I'd be able to get a few plants to grow. Out of my seedling list, I decided to indirect sow my sweet peppers, sunflowers, and tomatoes. After plopping one growing puck per cell, I filled the bottom of the tray with water and watched as the growing medium expanded. This took several minutes, but it allowed me time to mentally divide each starter kit and then label off which kit would contain which plant. Once the growth pellet went from brown "Watch it Grow" pills to what I'd consider more reasonable earth, I used a pair of chopsticks to make a divot into each cell, then transferred over a seed into each hole.

Was this level of care completely necessary? Probably not. Did it fill an evening? Definitely.

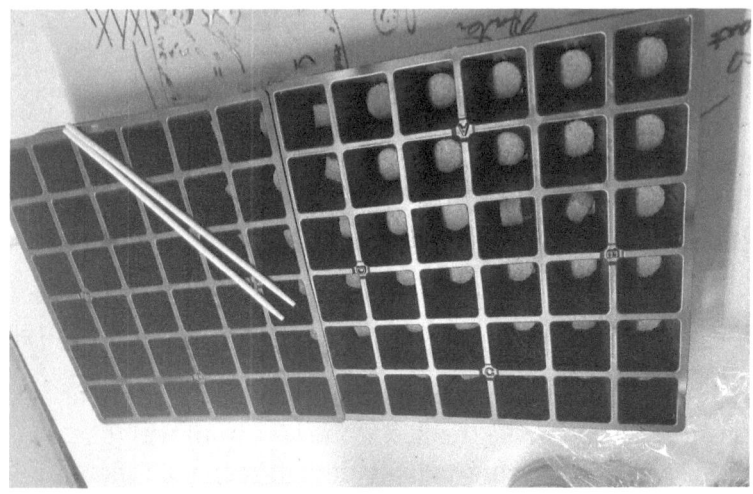

I then brought the trays up the two flights stairs to guest bedroom, refilled their water reservoirs, popped on the plastic tops and waited for the magic.

It didn't take long before I started to see signs of life in my back bedroom. My first indication was when condensation started to form on the inside of the growing lid. After a few days, I had my first shoots of green just pushing from the soil, and what seemed like the blink of an eye I had a massive amount of plants on my hands!

At first, I didn't know which seed tracker was which, because I when I labeled during the planting, the labels were only on my removable plastic tops. Luckily for me, peppers, sunflowers, and tomatoes all look very different from each other, even in seed form.

I started turning my seedlings every few days. They were lined up under my brightest window, but because it was their only light source the plants would tip towards the light and grow in one direction if left on their own. This would mean that when I transferred these plants into the ground, they wouldn't be as strong as possible and would have a tougher time surviving the transfer.

While all of this was going on, I did plant one seed packet basically as soon as it showed up. "French breakfast" radishes are are a small, oblong variety of radish that are usually pink or red in color with a white tip. They have a mild, slightly sweet flavor and a crisp texture, making them ideal for snacking or adding to salads. French breakfast radishes are typically harvested when they are young, before they become too spicy or woody. Because it's a feature to eat them young, the French breakfast radish has a maturity time of only 25 days. As the name implies, they're native to France, so they're well-suited to a Pittsburgh spring planting. The downside to planting a French breakfast radish is that they are *tiny* — you can pull a mature radish when it's barely six inches tall — but the entire thing is edible so that' a nice feature.

The small nature and quick growing cycle of my radishes in the cold, and the growth of my sunflowers, peppers, and tomatoes in the house demonstrated that I was on to something. Both direct and indirect sowing produced results, and as I snacked on my last French breakfast radish for the season, I was nearly ready to bring my roommates out of the house and into their new earthen home.

6. SUMMER

As the days grew longer and I reveled in my radishy success, I made further capital investments into my tiny backyard Eden. It became evident the rock garden and radish patch were not the only rocky spots in my yard. Because of the city life, my back yard is mostly landfill that over generations of time and topsoil, resembles "earth." Where there was once grass to hide, the planters showed me all of the pebble, nails, and glass that held my yard together. I have friends with bigger coffee tables than my planters, but I spent hours on my stomach sifting my soil one hand rake at a time. I wouldn't want to live in a space full of ancient bits of construction material, so why should my plants?

The inverse of the old adage, "out of sight, out of mind," is also evident in my front yard; my shoulder-height hedges make for a tempting target for sidewalk litter, so I make a habit of picking through the old soda bottles and beer cans that accumulate every few days. Every time I'm out there I think about some kind of sidewalk trash receptacle to encourage people not to litter, but I've never figured out a clever enough way to present an appropriate trash can.

It was during one of these musings that I struck up a conversation with my uphill neighbor. She commented on some of the work I was doing around the yard and offered some words of encouragement, then told me about the last major change she'd made to her yard. A few years before I moved in, our street got a new postal worker who took a new route than any previous mail delivery people. Instead of going up the stairs to the mailbox on the porch/down the stairs to the sidewalk/over from house to house, this delivery person would walk up the stairs then cut across yards. This saved considerable amounts of time and I thought it was a clever idea, but my neighbor pointed out this meant in warmer months we would have a mud pile next to our front entrances. One day while scraping mud off her shoes she had an idea: hostas.

Hostas are a perennial that come in a variety of colors, shapes, and sizes. They are shade-loving plants that prefer moist, well-drained soil and can thrive in many different climates. Hostas require basically zero maintenance after they take, and most varieties grow slowly. As if that doesn't make them great, hostas are also known to attract hummingbirds and other pollinators to the garden. As a kid I'd known them as "elephant plants" because of their broad leaves but they can come in smaller sizes too.

With the hostas, my neighbor had created the perfect timed natural barrier. They're perennials and follow a similar growth cycle to my rhubarb. Winters can be brutal in Pittsburgh and our postal workers serve a vital function, so during the cold months she's encouraged to use of the cut-through when the hostas are dormant underground. When "mud season" begins, the hostas return and the cut through is closed off. This might add extra steps, but it prevents a muddy tripping hazard and provides us some greenery, so I enthusiastically thanked her for telling me her tale and wondered if there was any kind of "defensive gardening" I could do to my yard.

Within the week I'd had my idea: I would add a trellis to the uphill garden in between the roses and the sage bush. A trellis is a structure to support climbing plants. They're typically made of wood, bamboo, metal, or plastic and can be either freestanding or attached to a wall or fence. The purpose of a trellis is to provide a framework for the plants to climb. You'll often find trellises used for things like grapes because it's easier to harvest the fruit and it helps mitigate rot. Trellising also helps to increase air circulation around the plants, which improves their overall health and reduces the risk of fungal infections. Additionally, trellising helps save space in the garden by allowing vertical growth, making it ideal for smaller plots or urban gardens. If I haven't already convinced you, they're also really cool looking on their own.

It was a moment of being a grumpy old person when I purchased my trellis. The four year old living next door started a new fun game of, "jump off of everything," and while the Children's Hospital of Pittsburgh is excellent, adding in some barriers between our yards felt like a sensible idea. When the trellis arrived and I started assembly in the back yard, he did show me his toy tool bag and offer assistance, so I told him when the trellis was up I'd make sure to plant a flower that was his favorite colors:

White and "puwple."

I thought purple flowers would make a striking contrast against the white of the trellis, so I acted on his suggestion. With my requirements being a perennial that can grow in full sun and a questionable soil type, I hit upon purple clematis as my trellis flower.

Depending on which variant chosen, clematis can grow as few as a few inches a year, or up to 20 feet in one year! One of the most important things when caring for clematis is that although the plant loves sun, their roots are fairly light sensitive. I selected a "medium growth" plant whose packaging claimed it would top out at around 12 feet tall. Clematis seeds can take up to three years before they really get into a vining mood, so I decided to go with a one-year-old nursery plant in an attempt to short-cut my dream of a full trellis. Once I planted my clematis, I added a layer of red mulch to the top. It definitely wasn't a requirement, but the red/white/green/purple of that corner just makes me happy.

I thought I'd have to go out and buy some white flowers to complete the color wheel of my neighbor's favorite colors, but I didn't have to make a purchase. Within the week of planting my clematis we'd be flooded with the smell and sight of some peculiar and brilliant white flowers coming from my front yard.

Through those first few months of homeownership, I didn't give much thought to the tree in my front yard. Roughly twelve feet tall and bounded to the edges of the hedge, it sits on the uphill end of my front yard. It's a tree in the strictest sense of the word — deciduous and woody enough it wasn't some freakish weed; tall enough it wasn't a shrub, but its scrawniness wasn't really something I thought added a huge amount of curb appeal. In winter it was downright ugly. I've passed by the tree on numerous occasions only to be thwacked in the face by a defoliated branch. These spindly branches do get their green fairly early in spring, and the tree fills out to the point it just blends in to the background, the sting of its wintry branches fading to memory. It's only for a brief window in early summer that my front yard tree breaks its banality to be an urban gardening gem; for my front yard is host to an elder tree.

Elder trees hold a sort of mysticism to them, but I never understood why until living with one. Native to North America, Asia, and Europe, some elder trees can grow to over 30 feet tall. Depending on where they grow, the elder tree develops its elderflowers in late spring or early summer. The flowers are tiny and a white/cream color. These tiny flowers extend off a common stalk into what's known as an umbel. The flowers smell incredible, with an almost musty honey smell, but each flower ripens on its own so some clusters can be past their bloom while others are just getting started. In Germany it's a delicacy to collect elderflower blooms and deep fry, served with a dusting of powered sugar. They're called *gebackene holunderblüten*, and the literal translation is "elderflower fritters."

I knew I had to do something with these magical flowers, but attempting a deep fry alone seemed a recipe for disaster, so I stumbled upon a sillier idea: elderflower liqueur. An incredibly popular cordial is the French St. Germain — they advertise as, "springtime in a bottle," so I started researching what a liqueur is in actuality. After some digging, a liqueur can be as simple as

neutral spirit + infusion + simple syrup

With my corner of glassware, access to vodka, sugar, and the stock for an infusion with my elderflower, I pushed forward with the thought experiment. In a stroke of genius I decided I had to attempt this when I thought of the name, **"St. GerMatt."**

Harvesting elderflower is a surreal experience. Bees love the scent, and because of the time of year they're in bloom, it seems that every bee in the county wants to stop in and take a whiff. All you need to harvest elderflower is a pair of scissors and a bucket to collect your flowers, but I learned some tricks quickly. Because of how small each flower is and how variable the bloom can be, you learn what ripe or unripe flowers feel like with the stroke of the back of your hand. The clustering nature of the elderflower means you can be as precise as you like when collecting. If a main artery isn't ready, you can still potentially collect a few flowers. You also learn to shake your flowers before popping them into your collection bucket. Working with nature always carries the risk of bringing bugs into your home, but without a good shake you're bound to bring in unwanted strays. No one likes to see bugs floating in their liqueur.

The liqueur making process is simple and fun. It's functionally the exact process of making a Southern-style sweet tea, except your base is vodka instead of water and you make your own tea bags in the form of cheesecloth-wrapped elderflower. The full recipe for my elderflower liqueur appears at the end of this book.

Conducting blind taste tests, and St. Germain and St. GerMatt are never mistaken as similar, and the St. GerMatt is divisive in my friend group: I think it's best served with a lemon seltzer as a cocktail, others dump it into a white wine sangria mix (which at that point can you even taste the flavors of a flower grown in my front yard?) Everyone is entitled to their opinion, but I take great joy in being able to share in something that's been processed from my yard.

Having barely made a small dent in my mason jar collection, I pivoted to growing in the back yard. I noticed there could be a pattern to all of this growing, and that I could have cohesion in how all of my plants and work fit together. So far, the best pattern or theme I could think of for my back yard was, "climbing."

A sun loving, fast climbing, explosive growing plant, the cucumber is an annual plant that is perfect for an urban gardener interested in growing their own vegetables.

Originally native to southeast Asia, the cucumber is a direct sow plant that can be placed in the garden after the danger of frost has passed — for Pittsburgh, this really means June. A creeping vine, after the seed sprouts the cucumber spreads out with spiraling tendrils. When these tendrils find a structure thin enough to wrap around, the plant grows its stalk in that direction.

Once the cucumber takes off, it produces broad, waxy leaves and then light-colored flowers. From the point the cucumber vine produces its first leaf to the end of its season, cucumbers love humidity, so keeping them hydrated is critical. The vegetable is 95% water, and you

can gain a newfound appreciation for how much water goes into producing food after growing your own cucumbers. That's not to say you can flood your garden; everything in moderation.

Leveraging the plant's tendril-then-grow behavior, thin metal supports are added to a a cucumber garden to control where the plant goes. I've seen people use chicken wire, or tomato cages, or other even other plants as the "staking" for cucumbers, but I went with a flat wire cage I found at my local hardware store. Flat caging means I can store my cages in my basement easily in the winter, and they can hook into each other to make 3D shapes to act as a tomato cage or similar garden barricade.

I set my cages to run perpendicular to my parking hole wall, and encouraged my cucumber vines up the cages. Their tendrils are fascinating but can be a little dumb, and it's not uncommon to see cucumber tendrils wrapped around another cucumber vine like a sloth that mistakes its own arm for a tree branch. Gentle encouragement with bread ties can go a long way to giving a cucumber the best chance possible.

Depending on the variety, five to ten weeks after first sow you'll have your first cucumber. The plant has been cultivated into a ton of different varieties that generally fall into the categories, "slicing," "seedless," and "pickling." Slicing cucumbers can grow to zucchini-level sizes, and are best eaten....sliced and raw, like in a simple salad or fancy sandwich. Some people believe cucumber seeds can make indigestion worse, so there are seedless cucumbers out there for growing. Because of their indigestion connection, seedless cucumbers can sometimes be called, "burpless cucumbers.

Pickling cucumbers are a variant that brings all different shapes, sizes, and flavors. Humans have been pickling things for thousands of years. All you need is your food, a container, and a preservation medium the food is submerged in to create an acidic environment that inhibits bacteria growth. Pickled cucumbers can range in size from the delicate cornichon to a state fair hand snack. Cucumbers bred for pickling also tend to have an upper bound on size — you won't really find a pickling cucumber that's bigger than the lid of a mason jar. The pickling process changes the vegetable, so a cucumber that gives a squeaky crunch as a pickle can be a bit tough when eaten raw.

When I think "pickle" I think "bread and butter," or "dill," and this word association is with the spices used in the pickling process. When I learned this, I decided that whatever my cucumber haul would be, I'd experiment with flavors once we got to pickling. I also limited myself to quick pickles — I didn't want to mess with a double boiler and the pasteurization process, and fermentation was equated to botulism in my mind at the time.

Three cages worth of plants in the garden netted me around twenty jars of pickles. I learned that "bread and butter" pickles are just...a small bit of every spice thrown into a jar with cucumbers, and that sage freshly picked from the garden turns to a pile of goo when simmered in hot vinegar, but it still imparts a flavor. I started with pickle chips, then transitioned to slicing into spears in the interest of preserving my sanity after I broke a jar smooshing cucumber slices on top of each other.

There's still a dent in my kitchen wall from where it bounced off before exploding on the floor.

Dubbing the fruits of my labor, **"Picklehalski Pickles,"** I made a few notes on some of the jars what spices went into which jar, then set them into my refrigerator for their cool down.

People went crazy for my Picklehalskis. My coworkers derided me for not turning my yard into a cucumber field, and my friends offered to start a barter economy in exchange for more pickles. My harshest critic came from my 90-year-old neighbor, who enjoyed the taste but said they were, "too crunchy for her teeth."

The cucumbers made me feel incredible on every level. Their need for humidity and vining nature meant they were never maintenance free, and that kept me in the in the garden and paying attention to my other plants. My peppers, sunflowers, pumpkins and pole beans were out in the yard and growing, and they all gave me things to marvel at in kind.

Gardening gives you an appreciation for the strength of life, but it also shows you its fragility. I love sweet peppers so I was excited for a bounty, but a cold snap after a transition from my back bedroom to the back yard meant my imagined pepper field in the rock garden was paltry pepper planter. Mis-timing when I first planted my seeds meant I'd wind up with a small yield of peppers. I think I only got one pepper per plant this year, and if I'm being honest, didn't taste any different from a grocery store pepper.

Similarly, I learned that sunflowers can be finicky when indirectly sown. Their tall nature means they grow a deep taproot — a root that pushes straight down to secure the plant before it goes into overdrive to reach its dramatic heights. When I transplanted my sunflowers, I was greeted to a nearly a dozen curled-up taproots that had themselves into their planting containers in my bedroom. Of the 30 seeds I started with, only one sunflower would grow to full bloom that first year. That singular sunflower was a joyful experience. The taller the sunflower, the longer a growing season required, so this was a "dwarf sunflower" that was only supposed to grow to five feet tall.

When the flower appeared, it was like a neon sign was lit for the creatures of Pittsburgh. Bees buzzed and fought around its yellowy flower, and small birds rested on its huge branches. As the flower faded, those birds found the seeds as an enticing snack, and squirrels started hanging out in its shade hoping for some oil-rich manna from heaven.

Every time I'd look out my kitchen window I'd see a new interaction. Because of this I asked my photographer friend to come over and take a picture of the sunflower. He said he'd have a photoshoot if I gave him two more jars of pickles. Seemed like a fair trade. After he picked through the remaining jars and selected the flavors he thought sounded most interesting, he snapped a few photos of the yard. I asked if he'd take a picture of me, and this, "Mattmerican Gothic" is my favorite photo taken of me.

My pumpkin was a slow burn. Pumpkins take a huge amount of time to reach maturity and I would't get a real pumpkin for a few more months. Their stalks amble and plod around the garden, going where they please. It's hard to tell when a pumpkin is going to shoot off in a direction and not produce a flower that will eventually become a pumpkin. It's harder still to gamble on which flowers to pluck and which to leave, playing god to your gourds and deciding which pumpkin lives and receives full nutrients from its plant and which are doomed to oblivion. Pumpkin harvesting season is in mid-fall for much of the northeast U.S., which is why we associate pumpkins with Halloween.

The pole beans were the final piece of my new planters. Growth from a bean stirs a magic learned in childhood. Everyone knows the story of Jack and the beanstalk, where a boy trades his last fortune to a wandering trader for "magic beans." The town thinks Jack a fool, until he plants the beans and they grow to reach the sky where giants live. You can't reach the sky with beans, but you can however choose from two variants of garden variety beans: pole beans and bush beans. They're both just green beans, but the main difference lies in their growing habits. At one to two feet tall, bush beans are compact and don't require any support. They produce a small crop in a shorter period of time — usually two to three weeks. Pole beans are those that grow taller, produce more, and take longer to develop. Some people say the extra growing time gives them a better flavor than their bushier cousins. They also require a structure to grow around, hence the name "pole bean.

Once bush beans are ruled out, one is presented with a myriad of pole bean varieties. I nearly purchased a variant called, "red runner" that was noted for its brilliant red flowers, but they were out of stock. I decided instead on a purple pole bean. After its white flowers bloom deep purple bean pods develop across the vine. Once the bean pod is opened their neon green flesh reveals a milky white bean.

These were a joy to grow. Planting the ghostly white bean knowing such greens and purples awaited was exciting, the vines were much more manageable than the cucumbers, and the plants produced beans in abundance. The four plants didn't yield a bushel or even a peck (antiquated and preposterous units for measuring produce,) but I did have a bounty of leftover beans. When storing beans to use for future planting, you want to keep them as dry as possible. Some people place their beans in their oven on the lowest setting to achieve this, but I just scooped some beans from their pods, washed and dried them, then left them on my kitchen counter on paper towels for a few days. They're ready when the beans have hardened to the point you can't leave a dent in the exterior with your fingernail. Popped into an airtight mason jar and stored in a dark place like a basement, the beans will be in perfect condition for next year's season.

Fortuitously I saved my purple pole beans, because like the mythical Jack I traded my beans for treasure. The local antique furniture store is a place I love to frequent — it's near a great coffee shop, the contents of the shop are always rotating, and the owners are incredibly friendly. On one visit to the store I struck up a conversation with the owner who mentioned she was planning her garden for the new house she'd moved into. She rotated her desktop monitor around and I excitedly reviewed her shopping cart of the seed supplier she had open in one of her tabs. I asked if the list was complete, we laughed at how you can never buy too many cool plants, and then she mentioned there was one plant that was out of stock. I told her about my struggle with the red runners and how I was excited for finding the purple pole beans, at which point she revealed she was looking for purple and they were nowhere to be found!

Dashing up the hill, I was back with my mason jar on the counter in under 10 minutes with a flabbergasted shopkeeper staring back at me. They were all hers to start her new garden. She asked if there was anything in particular I was looking for at their store, and I mentioned I needed a new coffee table but hadn't found anything at the moment. We parted ways and I left with nothing but the feeling of being neighborly.

Days passed and while listening to a podcast, a sensation of being watched came over me. Muting my distraction, I looked around to see I was walking in front of the antique furniture store and that the owner was shouting at me to come in. Apologizing for zoning out, I followed her into the back of the store and she showed me a really great looking coffee table. I said I love it and before I could ask her the price, she said they'd paid $20 at an estate sale for it and had just finished a refurb. The cost of the table (for me,) was $20 and the beans I'd given her. She even had my mason jar under her desk.

Recently a friend came across my exact coffee table while browsing the Internet: it turns out that thing is worth hundreds! I've convinced myself that coffee tables are the 21st century equivalent of a castle in the sky.

As the days grew shorter and the nights colder, I planned the next phase for my garden. The clematis crossed its second rung on the trellis, and I removed the cucumber and sunflower. I was sad to see them go, but excited for the next phase of my gardening journey; one that would bring every trick I had together into something greater than its parts.

7. FALL

A s the warm August rain cleared the city, a cool wind signaled the end of summer and the start of new planting opportunities. Before this year, I would have associated the change of seasons with an end to growing annuals, but the fall of 2020 proved that late-season planting can be fulfilling.

Though I cleared the uphill end of my new planter to make way for fall seeds, the contents of the downhill half were hitting their stride. I wish I took a picture of the juxtaposition, barren earth to the left and a small jungle to the right, separated only by a cairn of broken concrete.

The jungle nature of the downhill planter was entirely from my attempts at corralling the pumpkin. A squash, pumpkins have been grown in North America for over 9,000 years and have been an important crop as their seeds and flesh are tasty and beautiful. Being approximately 92% water, pumpkins require a healthy amount of watering and really prefer well draining soil; they don't root deeply, but root everywhere through arm-like vines. For some variants, pumpkin vines can grow at a rate of over one foot per day! The love of water, sprawling nature, and massive leaves makes a pumpkin a natural weed barrier — choking out any light to the ground but creating a humid environment to keep itself happy.

In August I made the decision about which small pumpkins would be the "chosen one." I was nearly going to select the first pumpkin to have developed when I noticed a yellow-orange smudge near the concrete pile. After pulling a leaf back, I had a gnarly looking pumpkin that was growing around bits of concrete.

This was my perfect pumpkin.

I rotated the pumpkin around the concrete pile and gave it a resting place in the grass. For the next few months until harvest, I rotated the pumpkin every few days.

Without rotation, pumpkins can be too heavy on one side or the other, leading to bursting. Leaving the pumpkin on its side a few days at a time allows the bottom of the pumpkin to breath — since you're frequently watering the plant the "fruit" of the pumpkin can get rotten if left in one place for too long. Frequent handling of the pumpkin also lets you understand if any pests are attempting to break into the goods on the inside — bugs, rodents, and birds can and will try to get to the sweet interior without some intervention.

Birds were hanging around my house more and more as the days become cooler. After shifting my pumpkin one late afternoon, I took a break and read for a while on my front porch. Rounding the corner of the house, I was greeted by nearly a hundred birds resting in my elder tree. After my heart rate normalized and the noise died down, I realized the birds were in the tree because it started to produce fruit.

Elderberries are small, purple fruits. They're seeded, and each springtime flower produces a single fruit. They look like if you crossed a cherry with a grape vine, then shrunk that down to one-tenth the original size. Elderberries are also rich in antioxidants and vitamins, and it's for this reason they've been used in home remedies for hundreds of years.

All this fun and benefit comes at a cost — unripe elderberries, the leaves, and stems and roots are all toxic if ingested. This is because the tree contains a large amount of cyanide. The berries also contain high amounts of lectin, a compound found in beans that can cause gastrointestinal discomfort.

The berries are edible once cooked. Harvesting elderberries is best done wearing gloves, as a crushed berry can leave a deep purple stain on one's fingers. Night after night, I dreamt I would produce an elderberry wine, but after I picked what I thought was a sensible amount of berries, leaving enough for the birds, I had less than a stellar yield. The cost of harvesting the flowers in spring meant I had few left to go to berry.

Scrapping the wine plan, I thought jelly would be a fun product to make. It seemed the next logical step after pickles. Jelly can be produced from garden-grown fruits, there are a million recipes online, and to make jelly you need to up-level your mason jar game with canning. I felt comfortable with the risks of boiling hot water and glass and set forth on my endeavor.

The results were not as I hoped. Even though I thought I followed the pectin instructions on the back of the packet, after the jelly cooled and was refrigerated I had less of a jelly and more of a thick syrup. The concoction was sweet and tart like a combination of a blueberry and a cherry, and it was great when drizzled on pancakes. I brought a few jars to Michigan on a work trip, and my coworker and his wife discovered the ultimate use for the jelly — a drizzle over Greek yogurt.

The last produce of the year took all of my growing to new heights: I wanted to grow and make my own kimchi.

A traditional Korean side dish, kimchi is a brined combination of vegetables that facto-ferment into a a spicy, tangy, and slightly sour condiment. This fermentation makes kimchi rich in probiotics and other beneficial nutrients, and it has been associated with various health benefits, including improved digestion, immune function, and heart health. Kimchi is highly adaptable — there are tons of recipes online for all different kimchis with different combinations of ingredients.

The way I think about kimchi is:

leafy plant + crunchy plant + sweet plant + spices = delicious

You'll see daikon radish, cucumbers, carrots, onions, and Napa cabbage as common ingredients in recipes across the internet. I decided cabbage and daikon would be my personal contribution to the kimchi. Daikon is similar to the red French breakfast radish I grew in spring, in that they're both radish and both grow during the cooler seasons. Daikon radish has a mild, slightly sweet taste, while red radishes have a sharper, spicier flavor. From a gardening perspective, the biggest difference is in their size. My biggest French breakfast radish was maybe the size of my thumb, but daikon get **big**. I picked a fairly run-of-the-mill seed pack of daikon and these were monsters when grown in my garden. Some of the smaller ones I snacked on the day I pulled them and they were ugly like a parsnip, but delicious.

The cabbage was less thrilling of a grow. Cabbages love a constant cool temperature, and their heads can split if exposed to too high or too cold a temperature. In milder

climates than Pittsburgh, they can be grown year-round, but I'm really limited to the spring and autumn like the rest of the Northeast and most of the Midwest. Cabbages love well draining, nitrogen rich soils, and my planter was actually a great growing medium for the plant. Previously covered in grass, the planter was really a great spot for the cabbage. Its rockiness likely contributed to the gnarling of my daikon, though.

I definitely did not monitor the cabbages close enough. Since they grow above ground, like pumpkins there are tons of pests who love to eat cabbages. With a pumpkin you have a brightly colored object you can turn over and inspect for damage. With cabbage, all kinds of burrowing and digging pests poke into the cabbage, which is a real pain.

My ratio of daikon to cabbage was way off, but I had enough cabbage I could at least say it would contribute some flavor. My friend Dan gave me a few apples from his back yard, and I decided that we'd have one batch of apple/daikon/cabbage kimchi, and one batch of carrot/daikon/cabbage kimchi to try.

The kimchi making process is a blast. Once you've cleaned and chopped your veggies and your brine solution is mixed, next you have the delightful task of brushing your

vegetables with your paste. An unused paintbrush really comes in handy to make sure you transfer over to the cabbage. Smooshing the vegetables into their jars is also an incredibly cathartic experience. Once jarred the red/white/green makes for a fascinating sight, like an incredibly slow moving lava lamp.

What's less fun is the part that comes next: facto-fermentation. The process acts to prolong your kimchi, but it means you leave your jar lids slightly open. Exposing the kimchi to the air allows for bacteria to come into the dish, and it allows gasses to be released without a pressure buildup. These jar farts also means your entire house will smell of...decaying vegetables for the entire time you have them out.

Stinking up my house was a labor of love. My friends all delighted in the kimchi, and I received pictures of the condiment in grilled cheese, in fried rice, or set next to gaming computers as a snack. We were still deeply in the pandemic and direct contact was difficult, but dropping off jars and receiving enthusiast feedback was an incredible gift.

The cabbage and daikon were my final annuals for the year. I still had the greenery of my bushes, but winter

quickly came and the green of the backyard faded to shade of brick and concrete.

I not only survived a year of pandemic, but thrived and learned new skills. Through gardening I improved my surroundings and brought new colors to my community. Through preparing the fruits of my garden, I cemented new connections with my neighbors and friends, and realized I could build upon skills and reach new heights of creativity. In taking my produce from the backyard to others' homes, I found a desire to do more.

To grow more. To learn more. To experiment with more; to be less afraid of failure and to document the steps along the way. As the new year approached, I cleaned my garden tools one final time for the year, and decided I would organize a photo album of the work I did through the year.

Organization, discovery, and growth. These were my takeaways from that first year of gardening, and I hope you enjoyed the journey. "To plant a garden is to believe in tomorrow," as Audrey Hepburn said, and each autumn I think back on this first gardening year. With Pittsburgh winter's bleakness, I focus on the belief in what tomorrow can become.

A Pandemic Gardening Journal

PART III :
SUPPLEMENTAL
INFORMATION

8. MATT'S TOP 10 URBAN GARDENING PLANTS FOR A MORE DRAMATIC YARD

1. Container corn
2. Purple pole beans
3. Cucumbers
4. Borage
5. Crocuses
6. Sunflower
7. Pumpkin
8. Hyacinth
9. Coneflower
10. Lavender

9. RHUBARB SYRUP

Ingredients:
- 2 cups chopped rhubarb
- 1 cup granulated sugar
- 1 cup water

Instructions:
1. Wash and chop the rhubarb into small pieces.
2. In a medium saucepan, combine the rhubarb, sugar, and water.
3. Bring the mixture to a boil over medium heat, stirring occasionally.
4. Once the mixture comes to a boil, reduce the heat to low and let it simmer for 20-25 minutes, or until the rhubarb has completely broken down and the liquid has thickened slightly.
5. Remove the saucepan from the heat and let the mixture cool for a few minutes.
6. Pour the mixture through a cheesecloth lined fine-mesh strainer into a heat-safe container, pressing down on the rhubarb with a spoon to extract as much liquid as possible.
7. Let the syrup cool to room temperature, then transfer it to a clean, airtight container.
8. Store the syrup in the refrigerator for up to 2 weeks.

Enjoy your homemade rhubarb simple syrup in cocktails, lemonades, or even drizzled over ice cream!

10. ELDERFLOWER LIQUEUR

Ingredients:
- 2 cups vodka
- 1 cup elderflowers, washed and dried
- 1 cup water
- 1 cup granulated sugar
- 1 lemon, sliced

Instructions:
1. In a large, sealable jar or bottle, combine the vodka and elderflowers.
2. Close the jar or bottle and let it steep for 2-3 days in a cool, dark place.
3. After 2-3 days, strain the mixture through a cheesecloth-lined fine mesh sieve to remove the elderflowers, and transfer the infused vodka back into the jar or bottle.
4. In a medium saucepan, combine the water, sugar, and lemon slices. Bring the mixture to a boil over medium heat, stirring occasionally to dissolve the sugar.
5. Once the sugar has dissolved and the mixture has come to a boil, reduce the heat to low and let it simmer for 5-10 minutes, or until the mixture has thickened slightly and the lemon slices have softened.
6. Remove the saucepan from the heat and let the syrup cool to room temperature.
7. Pour the syrup into the jar or bottle with the infused vodka, and stir to combine.
8. Close the jar or bottle and let it sit for another 2-3 days, stirring occasionally to ensure the flavors are fully incorporated.
9. After 2-3 days, strain the mixture through a fine-mesh sieve or cheesecloth to remove any solids or impurities, and transfer the liqueur to a clean, airtight container.

10. Store the liqueur in the refrigerator for up to 6 months.

Serve your homemade elderflower liqueur in cocktails, mixed drinks, or even as a flavorful addition to desserts!

11. MATT'S QUICK PICKLES

Ingredients:
- 2 medium cucumbers, sliced into rounds or spears
- 1 cup water
- 1 cup white vinegar
- 2 tablespoons granulated sugar
- 1 tablespoon kosher salt
- 1 tablespoon yellow mustard seed (optional)
- 1 teaspoon celery seed (optional)
- 1 teaspoon ground turmeric (optional)
- 1-2 cloves garlic, peeled and crushed (optional)
- 1 teaspoon dill seeds (optional)
- 4 fresh sage leaves, chopped (optional)
- Fresh dill sprigs (optional)

Instructions:
1. In a medium saucepan, combine the water, vinegar, sugar, salt, garlic, and dill seeds (if using). Bring the mixture to a boil over medium-high heat, stirring occasionally to dissolve the sugar and salt.
2. Once the mixture comes to a boil, remove the saucepan from the heat and let it cool for a few minutes.
3. Meanwhile, prepare your cucumbers by washing and slicing them into rounds or spears.
4. Pack the sliced cucumbers into a clean, heat-safe jar or container.
5. Pour the warm vinegar mixture over the cucumbers, making sure they are fully submerged.
6. Add a few sprigs of fresh dill (if using) to the jar or container.
7. Cover the jar or container with a lid or plastic wrap, and let it sit at room temperature for at least 1 hour, or until the pickles have reached your desired level of sourness.

8. Once the pickles are to your liking, transfer the jar or container to the refrigerator and let it chill for at least 1 hour before serving.
9. Enjoy your homemade cucumber pickles as a snack or as a flavorful addition to sandwiches and salads!

Note: These pickles will keep in the refrigerator for up to 2 weeks. The ingredients marked (optional) pair well together, and can be adjusted to taste.

12. ELDERBERRY JELLY

Ingredients:
- 3 cups elderberry juice
- 1 cup berry juice (optional)
- 1 package powdered pectin
- 4 cups granulated sugar
- Juice of 1/2 lemon

Instructions:
1. Rinse elderberries and remove stems.
2. Place elderberries in a large pot with 3 cups of water and bring to a boil. Reduce heat and simmer for 30-45 minutes, until berries are soft.
3. Mash berries with a potato masher or fork.
4. Strain berry mixture through a fine mesh sieve, cheesecloth, or jelly bag to remove solids and collect juice. You should have approximately 3 cups of juice.
5. In a separate pot, whisk together powdered pectin and 1/2 cup of sugar. Add elderberry juice and lemon juice and bring to a boil, stirring constantly.
6. Add remaining sugar and continue stirring until sugar is completely dissolved.
7. Boil mixture for 1-2 minutes, stirring constantly.
8. Remove pot from heat and skim any foam from the top of the jelly.
9. Ladle jelly into sterilized jars, leaving 1/4 inch of headspace. Wipe rims clean and screw on lids.
10. Process jars in a boiling water bath for 10 minutes.
11. Remove jars from water bath and let cool on a wire rack. Check seals after jars have cooled and store in a cool, dark place for up to a year.

Note: Jelly is based on a juice, so it's a bit hard to calculate how much elderberry you need to boil down for the required amount. It's possible to cut the elderberry with something like a blueberry, grape, or pomegranate juice, but if going this route make sure to find the no sugar added variant as the amount of sugar can interfere with the pectin packet.

13. FURTHER REFERENCES

If you're interested in checking out my tracking spreadsheets, drawings of the garden, and seed purchasing calculators, check out my GitHub page at:

https://github.com/mattpuchalski/garden

The page is updated regularly, especially in the winter and fall when I plan out my garden and then put my retrospective notes into the tracker!.

To determine the growing zone where you live, visit:

https://planthardiness.ars.usda.gov/

It's super easy to use and a lot of fun to play around and see how average temperatures can change over short distances.

ACKNOWLEDGEMENTS

Thank you to my family, friends, and coworkers who have put up with my constant talking about plants for the last few years. Thanks especially to Dan Swartz and Brian Margosian for your honest food reviews.

ABOUT THE AUTHOR

Matt Puchalski is an engineer based in Pittsburgh, Pennsylvania. Matt's work in the self-driving car space has seen his vehicles deployed across two continents. When not working, he can be found in his garden or in the local library.

An advocate for the community, Matt spends his free time promoting native plant species around Pittsburgh, and volunteering with the League of Women Voters.

To stay up-to-date on Matt's writing and other gardening tips, visit cononverln.com

www.ingramcontent.com/pod-product-compliance
Lightning Source LLC
Chambersburg PA
CBHW030505130626
46549CB00007B/2862